The UNITED STATES PRESIDENTS

Jimmy CARTER

Heidi M.D. Elston

Big Buddy Books

An Imprint of Abdo Publishing

abdopublishing.com

abdopublishing.com

Published by Abdo Publishing, a division of ABDO, PO Box 398166, Minneapolis, Minnesota 55439. Copyright © 2017 by Abdo Consulting Group, Inc. International copyrights reserved in all countries. No part of this book may be reproduced in any form without written permission from the publisher. Big Buddy Books™ is a trademark and logo of Abdo Publishing.

Printed in the United States of America, North Mankato, Minnesota
062016
092016

Design: Sarah DeYoung, Mighty Media, Inc.
Production: Mighty Media, Inc.
Editor: Rebecca Felix
Cover Photographs: Getty Images
Interior Photographs: AP Images (pp. 6, 15, 29); The Carter Center (p. 27); Corbis (pp. 5, 6, 9, 13, 17); Getty Images (p. 23); Courtesy: Jimmy Carter Library (pp. 7, 11, 25); Library of Congress (p. 19); Picture History (p. 21)

Cataloging-in-Publication Data

Names: Elston, Heidi M.D., author.
Title: Jimmy Carter / by Heidi M.D. Elston.
Description: Minneapolis, MN : Abdo Publishing, [2017] | Series: United States presidents | Includes bibliographical references and index.
Identifiers: LCCN 2015957283 | ISBN 9781680780871 (lib. bdg.) | ISBN 9781680775075 (ebook)
Subjects: LCSH: Carter, Jimmy, 1924- --Juvenile literature. | Presidents--United States--Biography--Juvenile literature. | United States--Politics and government--1977-1981--Juvenile literature.
Classification: DDC 973.926/092 [B]--dc23
LC record available at http://lccn.loc.gov/2015957283

Contents

Jimmy Carter

Jimmy Carter was the thirty-ninth US president. Carter believed in morality in government. He also believed the government should help the poor and the needy.

Carter was a simple man. He came from a small farm town in the Deep South. Voters trusted Carter. They felt comfortable with him.

After his presidency, Carter continued to give back to his country. He remained an example of honor and pride in America.

Timeline

1924

On October 1, James Earl Carter Jr. was born in Plains, Georgia.

1970

Carter was elected governor of Georgia.

1963

On January 14, Carter took office as a Georgia state senator.

1977

Carter took office as the thirty-ninth US president on January 20.

1978

Carter made history by arranging a meeting between Israeli **prime minister** Menachem Begin and Egyptian president Anwar Sadat.

1982

The Carter Center opened in Atlanta.

1999

Carter and his wife each received the Presidential Medal of Freedom.

2002

Carter received the **Nobel Peace Prize**.

Little Jimmy

James Earl Carter Jr. was born on October 1, 1924, in Plains, Georgia. He was known as Jimmy. He was the oldest son of James Earl Carter Sr. and Lillian Gordy Carter. Jimmy's father was a farmer. He grew corn, cotton, and peanuts.

★ FAST FACTS ★

Born: October 1, 1924

Wife: Eleanor Rosalynn Smith (1927–)

Children: four

Political Party: Democrat

Age at Inauguration: 52

Years Served: 1977–1981

Vice President: Walter Mondale

As a child, Jimmy earned one dollar a day selling boiled peanuts!

A Dream Fulfilled

Jimmy attended public schools in Plains. Then, in 1941, Jimmy attended Georgia Southwestern College. The next year, he entered the Georgia Institute of Technology.

Two years later, Jimmy entered the US Naval **Academy** in Annapolis, Maryland. He finished school in 1946. That same year, he married Eleanor Rosalynn Smith.

★ DID YOU KNOW? ★

Carter was the first US Naval Academy graduate to become a US president.

Carter and Eleanor Rosalynn Smith were married at Plains Methodist Church on July 7, 1946.

Family Man

Carter served as a naval officer for six years. Then, in 1953, his father died. At that time, James Earl Carter Sr. was a member of the Georgia House of **Representatives**. Carter decided he wanted to model his life after his father's.

To that end, Carter quit the navy and returned to Plains later that year. There, Carter served in local government. He was a member of the library and hospital boards. He also served on the school board.

Mrs. and Mr. Carter (*center*) with their family. The Carters had three sons and one daughter.

Election Recount

In 1962, Carter wanted to be **nominated** for the Georgia state senate. He lost the **primary** election to Homer Moore. But he lost by only 139 votes.

Carter believed Moore had won because of **fraud**. So, he fought the results. Carter asked that the votes be recounted.

After the recount, Carter was named the winner. He then won the general election too. Carter took office on January 14, 1963. He was reelected in 1964.

Carter (*fourth from left*) officially becoming a Georgia state senator

Governor Carter

Carter was elected governor of Georgia in 1970. He was different from most southern governors at that time. Carter was for **integration**. And, he appointed many African Americans to state government jobs.

Governor Carter traveled often. He also welcomed many international visitors. And, he met with leading national politicians. On December 12, 1974, Carter announced he would run for president.

Lillian Carter recalled learning her son wanted to run for president. He told her, "Momma, I'm going to run for president of the United States, and I'm going to win."

Scandal

In 1972, a huge **scandal** occurred. On June 17, police arrested five men. They had broken into the Watergate building in Washington, DC. They were there to steal secrets to help President Richard Nixon's reelection campaign.

At first, Nixon said he had nothing to do with it. But on August 9, he left office. Vice President Gerald Ford became president. But Ford's popularity dropped when he **pardoned** Nixon. This would help Carter in the next presidential election.

Nixon said he didn't know about the Watergate break-in. His famous quote about it is "I am not a crook."

The 1976 Election

In 1976, the **Democrats** chose Carter to run for president. Carter was not well-known. But, he appealed to many different kinds of people. He promised to improve the government.

On November 2, Carter won. He earned 297 **electoral votes**. Ford received 240. This was the closest presidential election in more than 60 years.

Carter campaigned as an honest and trustworthy man.

President Carter

On January 20, 1977, Carter became the thirty-ninth US president. That winter, the nation faced a natural gas shortage. People needed natural gas to heat their homes. So, Carter asked Congress to pass a plan. It would send natural gas to areas with shortages.

Another concern was the US **economy**. Many Americans were without jobs. And prices for food, clothes, and houses were high. Carter worked to improve the economy, but expenses continued to increase.

PRESIDENT CARTER'S CABINET

January 20, 1977–January 20, 1981

- ★ **STATE:** Cyrus Vance,
  Edmund S. Muskie (from May 8, 1980)
- ★ **TREASURY:** W. Michael Blumenthal,
  George W. Miller (from August 6, 1979)
- ★ **DEFENSE:** Harold Brown
- ★ **ATTORNEY GENERAL:** Griffin B. Bell,
  Benjamin R. Civiletti (from August 16, 1979)
- ★ **INTERIOR:** Cecil Dale Andrus
- ★ **AGRICULTURE:** Robert S. Bergland
- ★ **COMMERCE:** Juanita M. Kreps,
  Philip M. Klutznick (from January 9, 1980)
- ★ **LABOR:** F. Ray Marshall
- ★ **HEALTH, EDUCATION, AND WELFARE:**
  Joseph A. Califano Jr.,
  Patricia Roberts Harris (from August 3, 1979)
- ★ **HEALTH AND HUMAN SERVICES:**
  Patricia Roberts Harris (from September 27, 1979)
- ★ **HOUSING AND URBAN DEVELOPMENT:**
  Patricia Roberts Harris,
  Moon Landrieu (from September 24, 1979)
- ★ **TRANSPORTATION:** Brock Adams,
  Neil E. Goldschmidt (from September 24, 1979)
- ★ **ENERGY:** James R. Schlesinger (from October 1, 1977),
  Charles W. Duncan Jr. (from August 24, 1979)
- ★ **EDUCATION:** Shirley M. Hufstedler
  (from December 6, 1979)

23

Foreign Affairs

President Carter had better success helping **foreign** countries. He traveled to many different continents. There, he **promoted** world peace.

In 1978, President Carter made history. He arranged a meeting between the Israeli **prime minister** and Egyptian president. The two leaders agreed to create a peace **treaty**.

Then trouble struck. In 1979, the US **embassy** in Iran was seized. More than 50 Americans were taken captive. They were not freed until after Carter left office in 1981.

Egyptian president Anwar Sadat (*left*), Carter, and Israeli prime minster Menachem Begin (*right*)

A True Leader

After leaving the White House, Carter returned to Plains. He served as a professor at Emory University in Atlanta, Georgia. He also wrote more than 20 books.

Mr. and Mrs. Carter founded The Carter Center in 1982. It is in Atlanta. The center works to fight sickness, **poverty**, and hunger throughout the world.

Carter still travels to many countries. He **promotes** world peace and helps solve world problems.

Carter continues to travel around the world to promote good health.

In 1999, Mr. and Mrs. Carter each received the Presidential Medal of Freedom. This is the nation's highest honor for nonmilitary people.

Then in 2002, Carter received the **Nobel Peace Prize**. Each year, this prize is given to a person who works for world peace.

In 2015, Carter got **cancer**. Within a year, he was successfully treated. But doctors continue to watch his health.

Carter worked hard for many years and accomplished much. From naval officer to president, he truly led by example. Today, Jimmy Carter remains a leader.

After his presidency, Carter traveled the world giving speeches. In February 2016, he gave a speech to British leaders in London, England.

Office of the President

Branches of Government

The US government has three branches. They are the executive, legislative, and judicial branches. Each branch has some power over the others. This is called a system of checks and balances.

★ Executive Branch

The executive branch enforces laws. It is made up of the president, the vice president, and the president's cabinet. The president represents the United States around the world. He or she also signs bills into law and leads the military.

★ Legislative Branch

The legislative branch makes laws, maintains the military, and regulates trade. It also has the power to declare war. This branch includes the Senate and the House of Representatives. Together, these two houses form Congress.

★ Judicial Branch

The judicial branch interprets laws. It is made up of district courts, courts of appeals, and the Supreme Court. District courts try cases. Sometimes people disagree with a trial's outcome. Then he or she may appeal. If a court of appeals supports the ruling, a person may appeal to the Supreme Court.

Qualifications for Office

To be president, a candidate must be at least 35 years old. The person must be a natural-born US citizen. He or she must also have lived in the United States for at least 14 years.

Electoral College

The US presidential election is an indirect election. Voters from each state choose electors. These electors represent their state in the Electoral College. Each elector has one electoral vote. Electors cast their vote for the candidate with the highest number of votes from people in their state. A candidate must receive the majority of Electoral College votes to win.

Term of Office

Each president may be elected to two four-year terms. The presidential election is held on the Tuesday after the first Monday in November. The president is sworn in on January 20 of the following year. At that time, he or she takes the oath of office.
It states:

> I do solemnly swear (or affirm) that I will faithfully execute the office of President of the United States, and will to the best of my ability, preserve, protect and defend the Constitution of the United States.

31

Line of Succession

The Presidential Succession Act of 1947 states who becomes president if the president cannot serve. The vice president is first in the line. Next are the Speaker of the House and the President Pro Tempore of the Senate. It may happen that none of these individuals is able to serve. Then the office falls to the president's cabinet members. They would take office in the order in which each department was created:

Secretary of State

Secretary of the Treasury

Secretary of Defense

Attorney General

Secretary of the Interior

Secretary of Agriculture

Secretary of Commerce

Secretary of Labor

Secretary of Health and Human Services

Secretary of Housing and Urban Development

Secretary of Transportation

Secretary of Energy

Secretary of Education

Secretary of Veterans Affairs

Secretary of Homeland Security

Benefits

★ While in office, the president receives a salary. It is $400,000 per year. He or she lives in the White House. The president also has 24-hour Secret Service protection.

★ The president may travel on a Boeing 747 jet. This special jet is called Air Force One. It can hold 70 passengers. It has kitchens, a dining room, sleeping areas, and more. Air Force One can fly halfway around the world before needing to refuel. It can even refuel in flight!

★ When the president travels by car, he or she uses Cadillac One. It is a Cadillac Deville that has been modified. The car has heavy armor and communications systems. The president may even take Cadillac One along when visiting other countries.

★ The president also travels on a helicopter. It is called Marine One. It may also be taken along when the president visits other countries.

★ Sometimes the president needs to get away with family and friends. Camp David is the official presidential retreat. It is located in Maryland. The US Navy maintains the retreat. The US Marine Corps keeps it secure. The camp offers swimming, tennis, golf, and hiking.

★ When the president leaves office, he or she receives lifetime Secret Service protection. He or she also receives a yearly pension of $203,700. The former president also receives money for office space, supplies, and staff.

PRESIDENTS AND THEIR TERMS

PRESIDENT	PARTY	TOOK OFFICE	LEFT OFFICE	TERMS SERVED	VICE PRESIDENT
George Washington	None	April 30, 1789	March 4, 1797	Two	John Adams
John Adams	Federalist	March 4, 1797	March 4, 1801	One	Thomas Jefferson
Thomas Jefferson	Democratic-Republican	March 4, 1801	March 4, 1809	Two	Aaron Burr, George Clinton
James Madison	Democratic-Republican	March 4, 1809	March 4, 1817	Two	George Clinton, Elbridge Gerry
James Monroe	Democratic-Republican	March 4, 1817	March 4, 1825	Two	Daniel D. Tompkins
John Quincy Adams	Democratic-Republican	March 4, 1825	March 4, 1829	One	John C. Calhoun
Andrew Jackson	Democrat	March 4, 1829	March 4, 1837	Two	John C. Calhoun, Martin Van Buren
Martin Van Buren	Democrat	March 4, 1837	March 4, 1841	One	Richard M. Johnson
William H. Harrison	Whig	March 4, 1841	April 4, 1841	Died During First Term	John Tyler
John Tyler	Whig	April 6, 1841	March 4, 1845	Completed Harrison's Term	Office Vacant
James K. Polk	Democrat	March 4, 1845	March 4, 1849	One	George M. Dallas
Zachary Taylor	Whig	March 5, 1849	July 9, 1850	Died During First Term	Millard Fillmore

PRESIDENT	PARTY	TOOK OFFICE	LEFT OFFICE	TERMS SERVED	VICE PRESIDENT
Millard Fillmore	Whig	July 10, 1850	March 4, 1853	Completed Taylor's Term	Office Vacant
Franklin Pierce	Democrat	March 4, 1853	March 4, 1857	One	William R.D. King
James Buchanan	Democrat	March 4, 1857	March 4, 1861	One	John C. Breckinridge
Abraham Lincoln	Republican	March 4, 1861	April 15, 1865	Served One Term, Died During Second Term	Hannibal Hamlin, Andrew Johnson
Andrew Johnson	Democrat	April 15, 1865	March 4, 1869	Completed Lincoln's Second Term	Office Vacant
Ulysses S. Grant	Republican	March 4, 1869	March 4, 1877	Two	Schuyler Colfax, Henry Wilson
Rutherford B. Hayes	Republican	March 3, 1877	March 4, 1881	One	William A. Wheeler
James A. Garfield	Republican	March 4, 1881	September 19, 1881	Died During First Term	Chester Arthur
Chester Arthur	Republican	September 20, 1881	March 4, 1885	Completed Garfield's Term	Office Vacant
Grover Cleveland	Democrat	March 4, 1885	March 4, 1889	One	Thomas A. Hendricks
Benjamin Harrison	Republican	March 4, 1889	March 4, 1893	One	Levi P. Morton
Grover Cleveland	Democrat	March 4, 1893	March 4, 1897	One	Adlai E. Stevenson
William McKinley	Republican	March 4, 1897	September 14, 1901	Served One Term, Died During Second Term	Garret A. Hobart, Theodore Roosevelt

PRESIDENT	PARTY	TOOK OFFICE	LEFT OFFICE	TERMS SERVED	VICE PRESIDENT
Theodore Roosevelt	Republican	September 14, 1901	March 4, 1909	Completed McKinley's Second Term, Served One Term	Office Vacant, Charles Fairbanks
William Taft	Republican	March 4, 1909	March 4, 1913	One	James S. Sherman
Woodrow Wilson	Democrat	March 4, 1913	March 4, 1921	Two	Thomas R. Marshall
Warren G. Harding	Republican	March 4, 1921	August 2, 1923	Died During First Term	Calvin Coolidge
Calvin Coolidge	Republican	August 3, 1923	March 4, 1929	Completed Harding's Term, Served One Term	Office Vacant, Charles Dawes
Herbert Hoover	Republican	March 4, 1929	March 4, 1933	One	Charles Curtis
Franklin D. Roosevelt	Democrat	March 4, 1933	April 12, 1945	Served Three Terms, Died During Fourth Term	John Nance Garner, Henry A. Wallace, Harry S. Truman
Harry S. Truman	Democrat	April 12, 1945	January 20, 1953	Completed Roosevelt's Fourth Term, Served One Term	Office Vacant, Alben Barkley
Dwight D. Eisenhower	Republican	January 20, 1953	January 20, 1961	Two	Richard Nixon
John F. Kennedy	Democrat	January 20, 1961	November 22, 1963	Died During First Term	Lyndon B. Johnson
Lyndon B. Johnson	Democrat	November 22, 1963	January 20, 1969	Completed Kennedy's Term, Served One Term	Office Vacant, Hubert H. Humphrey
Richard Nixon	Republican	January 20, 1969	August 9, 1974	Completed First Term, Resigned During Second Term	Spiro T. Agnew, Gerald Ford

PRESIDENT	PARTY	TOOK OFFICE	LEFT OFFICE	TERMS SERVED	VICE PRESIDENT
Gerald Ford	Republican	August 9, 1974	January 20, 1977	Completed Nixon's Second Term	Nelson A. Rockefeller
Jimmy Carter	Democrat	January 20, 1977	January 20, 1981	One	Walter Mondale
Ronald Reagan	Republican	January 20, 1981	January 20, 1989	Two	George H.W. Bush
George H.W. Bush	Republican	January 20, 1989	January 20, 1993	One	Dan Quayle
Bill Clinton	Democrat	January 20, 1993	January 20, 2001	Two	Al Gore
George W. Bush	Republican	January 20, 2001	January 20, 2009	Two	Dick Cheney
Barack Obama	Democrat	January 20, 2009	January 20, 2017	Two	Joe Biden

"I say to you quite frankly that the time for racial discrimination is over."

Jimmy Carter

★ WRITE TO THE PRESIDENT ★

You may write to the president at:
The White House
1600 Pennsylvania Avenue NW
Washington, DC 20500

You may e-mail the president at:
comments@whitehouse.gov

37

Glossary

academy—a private school that trains students in a certain field.

cancer—any of a group of very harmful diseases that cause a body's cells to become unhealthy.

Democrat—a member of the Democratic political party.

economy—the way that a country produces, sells, and buys goods and services.

electoral vote—a vote cast by a member of the Electoral College for the candidate who received the most popular votes in his or her state.

embassy—the home and offices of an ambassador in a foreign country.

foreign—located outside one's own country.

fraud—a crime in which someone cheats to gain something valuable for himself or herself.

inauguration (ih-naw-gyuh-RAY-shuhn)—a ceremony in which a person is sworn into office.

integration—opening public places and organizations to people of all races.

Nobel Peace Prize—an award given for doing something to help make peace in the world.

nominate—to name as a possible winner.

pardon—to free a person from punishment for an offense.

poverty—the state of being poor.

primary—an election before the main election in which members of the same political party run against each other. Voters choose candidates to run in the main election.

prime minister—the head of the government in some countries.

promote—to help something happen, develop, or increase.

representative—someone chosen in an election to act or speak for the people who voted for him or her.

scandal—an action that shocks people and disgraces those connected with it.

treaty—an agreement made between two or more groups.

WEBSITES

To learn more about the US Presidents, visit **booklinks.abdopublishing.com**. These links are routinely monitored and updated to provide the most current information available.

Index

31901059790016